Water changes

Bobbie Kalman

🌳 **Crabtree Publishing Company**

www.crabtreebooks.com

Created by Bobbie Kalman

Author and Editor-in-Chief
Bobbie Kalman

Educational consultants
Elaine Hurst
Joan King
Jennifer King

Notes for adults
Jennifer King

Editors
Kathy Middleton
Crystal Sikkens

Design
Bobbie Kalman
Katherine Berti

Print and production coordinator
Katherine Berti

Prepress technician
Katherine Berti

Photo research
Bobbie Kalman

Photographs by Shutterstock

Library and Archives Canada Cataloguing in Publication

Kalman, Bobbie, 1947-
    Water changes / Bobbie Kalman.

(My world)
Issued also in electronic format.
ISBN 978-0-7787-9559-9 (bound).--ISBN 978-0-7787-9584-1 (pbk.)

    1. Hydrologic cycle--Juvenile literature. 2. Water--Juvenile literature. I. Title. II. Series: My world (St. Catharines, Ont.)

GB848.K335 2011   j551.48   C2010-907438-6

Library of Congress Cataloging-in-Publication Data

Kalman, Bobbie.
  Water changes / Bobbie Kalman.
      p. cm. -- (My world)
  ISBN 978-0-7787-9584-1 (pbk. : alk. paper) -- ISBN 978-0-7787-9559-9 (reinforced library binding : alk. paper) -- ISBN 978-1-4271-9666-8 (electronic (pdf))
  1. Hydrologic cycle--Juvenile literature. 2. Water--Juvenile literature. I. Title. II. Series.

  GB848.K35 2011
  551.48--dc22
                                        2010047123

Crabtree Publishing Company
www.crabtreebooks.com   1-800-387-7650

Printed in the U.S.A./102016/CG20160822

Published in Canada
Crabtree Publishing
616 Welland Ave.
St. Catharines, Ontario
L2M 5V6

Published in the United States
Crabtree Publishing
PMB 59051
350 Fifth Avenue, 59th Floor
New York, New York 10118

Published in the United Kingdom
Crabtree Publishing
Maritime House
Basin Road North, Hove
BN41 1WR

Published in Australia
Crabtree Publishing
3 Charles Street
Coburg North
VIC, 3058

Words to know

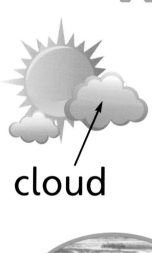
cloud

freezes

ice
(solid)

liquid

mist

ocean

rain

snow

vapor

water
cycle

If you look at Earth, you will see that most of it is blue. The blue parts are water. Most of the water on Earth is in **oceans**.

Atlantic Ocean

Pacific Ocean

Oceans are huge areas of water.
Name two oceans.

The water on Earth changes.
It changes when it gets warmer.
It changes when it gets colder.
Water can be **liquid**, **solid**, or **vapor**.

water vapor

Liquid water is the water you drink. You can swim in it and wash with it. This girl is swimming in liquid water.

liquid water

When water gets very cold, it **freezes** into **ice** or **snow**.

Ice is solid water. It is cold and hard.

ice

ice

Snow is solid water, too,
but it is not as hard as ice.
You can make a snowman with it.

snow

snowman

When water is heated by the sun, it becomes water vapor. Water vapor is all around you, even if you cannot see it.

Sometimes you can see
water vapor in the air.
It is called **mist**.

mist

The wind takes water vapor
high into the sky.
It is colder high in the sky.
The vapor cools and
forms **clouds**.

clouds

Water falls from the clouds as **rain**.
Rain is liquid water.
What falls from clouds in winter?

Water is always changing.
It moves up to the sky.
It falls back down to Earth.
Water moving up to the sky
and back down to Earth
is called the **water cycle**.

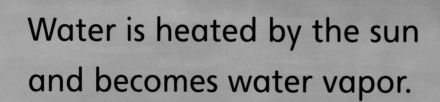

Water is heated by the sun
and becomes water vapor.

cloud

Water falls from
the clouds as rain
or snow.

Water vapor moves
up to the sky
and forms clouds.

rain snow

Snow melts and
becomes liquid water.

Notes for adults

Objective
- to have children share how they feel about different water experiences
- to introduce children to the concept of how water changes and becomes part of the water cycle

Before reading
Ask the children:
"Who likes to swim? When do you swim?"
"Who likes to play in puddles? When can you play in puddles?"
"Who likes to make snowmen? When can you make snowmen?"
"When is it difficult to see far outside?" (When there is fog or mist.)
Bring in different forms of water—ice, warm water, cold water, vapor from a boiling kettle of water, and snow. (You can use cotton balls to make snow. Try adding a little water so it looks more like snow.) Ask the children how each one looks and feels. Try to elicit words such as freezing, hot, misty or foggy, cold, and lukewarm.

Questions after reading the book
"How does water change?"
"When is water a liquid?"
"What can you do in or with liquid water?"
"What are oceans? Can you name two?"
"When is water a solid?"
"What do you do when it rains?"
"What do you like to do when it snows?"
"When does water turn to ice?"
"What would happen if you put a snowball into the freezer?"

Activity
Make some popsicles with the children. Pour juice or flavored water into ice-cube trays and freeze overnight. Ask the children what solid water feels like in their mouths. (cold, hard) Bring in a kettle and let it boil. How does water vapor look? Ask the children to think of words to describe the vapor. Ask them where they can find vapor in their homes (after a hot shower) or outdoors (mist and fog).

Extension
With the help of the children, make up a song about the water cycle. Sing it to the tune of "I'm a Little Teapot."
The water is in oceans. They are huge.
When the Earth heats up, they do, too.
The water becomes vapor and rises high, forming clouds up in the sky.
The water falls down as rain or snow.
I put on my raincoat when rain starts to flow.
When the water falls down and there is snow,
I get my toboggan and down a hill I go!

For teacher's guide, go to www.crabtreebooks.com/teachersguides